Planning for Learning through The Environment

by Rachel Sparks Linfield Illustrated by Cathy Hughes

Contents

Published by Practical Pre-School Books
MA Education, Dulwich Road, Herne Hill, London, SE24 0PB Tel: 020 7738 5454
© MA Education 2009   www.practicalpreschoolbooks.com

Planning for Learning through The Environment ISBN: 978 1 90457 582 5

Making plans

Why plan?

The purpose of planning is to make sure that all children enjoy a broad and balanced curriculum. All planning should be useful. Plans are working documents that you spend time preparing, which later should repay your efforts. Try to be concise. This will help you to find information quickly when you need it.

Long-term plans

Preparing a long-term plan, which maps out the curriculum during a year or even two, will help you to ensure that you are providing a variety of activities and are meeting the *Statutory Framework for the Early Years Foundation Stage* (2007).

Your long-term plan need not be detailed. Divide the time period over which you are planning into fairly equal sections such as half terms. Choose a topic for each section. Young children benefit from making links between the new ideas they encounter so, as you select each topic, think about the time of year in which you plan to do it. A topic about minibeasts will not be very successful in November!

Although each topic will address all the learning areas, some could focus on a specific area. For example,

a topic on Environments would lend itself well to activities relating to Problem Solving, Reasoning and Numeracy and Knowledge and Understanding of the World. Another topic might particularly encourage the appreciation of stories. Try to make sure that you provide a variety of topics in your long-term plans such as:

Autumn 1	Nursery Rhymes
Autumn 2	Shoppping / Christmas
Spring 1	Space
Spring 2	Food
Summer 1	The Environment
Summer 2	The Sea

Medium-term plans

Medium-term plans will outline the contents of a topic in a little more detail. One way to start this process is by making a spider-diagram on a large piece of paper. Work with your team writing down all the activities you can think of which are relevant to the topic. As you do this it may become clear that some activities go well together. Think about dividing them into themes. The topic of 'the Environment', for example, has themes such as 'My environment', 'Taking care of the environment', 'Clean up week', 'Rainforests', 'Hot deserts' and 'Cold deserts'. At this stage it is helpful to make a chart. Write the theme ideas down the side of the chart and put a different area of learning at the top of each column. Now you can insert your ideas and will quickly see where there are gaps. As you complete the chart take account of children's earlier experiences and provide opportunities for them to progress.

Refer back to the *Statutory Framework for the Early Years Foundation Stage* and check that you have addressed as many different aspects of it as you can. Once all your medium-term plans are complete make sure that there are no neglected areas.

Day-to-day plans

The plans you make for each day will outline aspects such as:
- resources needed;
- the way in which you might introduce activities;

Planning
for Learning
through
The
Environment

2   Practical Pre-School Books

Making plans

Ryan is going around the world...

- individual needs;
- the organisation of adult help;
- size of the group;
- timing;
- safety;
- key vocabulary.

Identify the learning and the ELGs that each activity is intended to promote. Make a note of any assessments or observations that you are likely to carry out. After carrying out the activities, make notes on your plans to say what was particularly successful, or any changes you would make another time.

A final note

Planning should be seen as flexible. Not all groups meet every day, and not all children attend every day. Any part of the plan can be used independently, stretched over a longer period or condensed to meet the needs of any group. You will almost certainly adapt the activities as children respond to them in different ways and bring their own ideas, interests and enthusiasms. The important thing is to ensure that the children are provided with a varied and enjoyable curriculum that meets their individual developing needs.

Using the book

- Collect or prepare suggested resources as listed on page 21.
- Read the section which outlines links to the Early Learning Goals (pages 4 - 7) and explains the rationale for the topic of 'the Environment'.
- For each weekly theme two activities are described in detail as an example to help you in your planning and preparation. Key vocabulary, questions and learning opportunities are identified.
- The skills chart on page 23 will help you to see at a glance which aspects of children's development are being addressed as a focus each week.
- As children take part in the topic activities, their learning will progress. Collecting Evidence on page 22 explains how you might monitor children's achievements.

- Find out on page 20 how the topic can be brought together in an Environmental Patchwork Day to involve carers, children and friends.
- There is additional material to support the working partnership of families and children in the form of a Home Links page, and a photocopiable Parents' Page found at the back of the book.

It is important to appreciate that the ideas presented in this book will only be a part of your planning. Many activities that will be taking place as routine in your group may not be mentioned. For example, it is assumed that sand, dough, water, puzzles, floor toys and large scale apparatus are part of the ongoing early years experience, as are the opportunities for children to develop ICT skills. Role-play areas, stories, rhymes, singing, and group discussion times are similarly assumed to be happening in each week although they may not be a focus for described activities. Groups should also ensure that there is a balance of adult-led and child-initiated activities.

Using this book in Northern Ireland, Scotland and Wales

Although the curriculum guidelines in Northern Ireland, Scotland and Wales differ, the activities in this book are still appropriate for use throughout the United Kingdom. They are designed to promote the development of early skills and to represent good practice in the early years

Glossary

EYFS: Early Years Foundation Stage
ELG: Early Learning Goal

Using the 'Early Learning Goals'

Having chosen your topic and made your medium-term plans you can use the Statutory Framework for the Early Years Foundation Stage to highlight the key learning opportunities your activities will address. **The Early Learning Goals are split into six areas: Personal, Social and Emotional Development; Communication, Language and Literacy; Problem Solving, Reasoning and Numeracy; Knowledge and Understanding of the World; Physical Development and Creative Development. Do not expect each of your topics to cover every goal but your long-term plans should allow for all of them to be addressed by the time a child enters Year 1.**

The following section gives the Early Learning Goals in point form to show what children are expected to be able to do in each area of learning by the time they enter Year 1. These points will be used throughout this book to show how activities for a topic on 'Environments' link to these expectations. For example Personal, Social and Emotional Development point 7 is 'form good relationships with adults and peers'. Activities suggested which provide the opportunity for children to do this will have the reference PS7. This will enable you to see which parts of the Early Learning Goals are covered in a given week and plan for areas to be revisited and developed.

In addition you can ensure that activities offer variety in the goals to be encountered. Often an activity may be carried out to achieve different Early LearningGoals. For instance, during this topic children will look

for picture books that have pictures of areas similar to their local environment. Children will develop their knowledge and understanding of the world as they identify features. In addition, they will develop in the area of Communication, Language and Literacy as they share books, attempt to read words, speak and listen. It is important, therefore, that activities have clearly defined goals so that these may be emphasised during the activity and for recording purposes.

Personal, Social and Emotional Development (PS)

This area of learning covers important aspects of development that affect the way children learn, behave and relate to others. By the end of the Early Years Foundation Stage (EYFS) children should:

PS1 Continue to be interested, excited and motivated to learn.

PS2 Be confident to try new activities, initiate ideas and speak in a familiar group.

PS3 Maintain attention, concentrate, and sit quietly when appropriate.

PS4 Respond to significant experiences, showing a range of feelings when appropriate.

PS5 Have a developing awareness of their own needs, views and feelings, and be sensitive to the needs, views and feelings of others.

PS6 Have a developing respect for their own cultures and beliefs and those of other people.

PS7 Form good relationships with adults and peers.

PS8 Work as a part of a group or class, taking turns and sharing fairly, understanding that there needs to be agreed values and codes of behaviour for groups of people, including adults and children, to work together harmoniously.

PS9 Understand what is right, what is wrong and why.

PS10 Consider the consequences of their words and actions for themselves and others.

PS11 Dress and undress independently and mange their own personal hygiene.

PS12 Select and use activities and resources independently.

PS13 Understand that people have different needs, views, cultures and beliefs, that need to be treated with respect.

PS14 Understand that they can expect others to treat their needs, views, cultures and beliefs with respect.

The topic of 'The Environment' offers many opportunities for children's personal, social and emotional development. Times spent discussing features of environments and clothes to wear in different settings will encourage children to speak in a group and to be interested to learn. Through looking at pictures of deserts and rainforests and talking about interesting facts the children will be motivated to learn. Many of the goals outlined above, though, will be covered on an almost incidental basis as children carry out the activities described in this book for the other areas of children's learning. During undirected free choice times they will be developing PS12 whilst any small group activity that involves working with an adult will help children to work towards PS7. Throughout all their work on environments the children should be encouraged to appreciate the need to take care of their immediate locality and the wider world.

Communication, Language and Literacy (L)

By the end of the EYFS, children should:

L1 Interact with others, negotiating plans and activities and taking turns in conversation.
L2 Enjoy listening to and using spoken and written language, and readily turn to it in their play and learning.
L3 Sustain attentive listening, responding to what they have heard with relevant comments, questions or actions.
L4 Listen with enjoyment, and respond to stories, songs and other music, rhymes and poems and make up their own stories, songs, rhymes and poems.
L5 Extend their vocabulary, exploring the meanings and sounds of new words.
L6 Speak clearly and audibly with confidence and control and show awareness of the listener.
L7 Use language to imagine and recreate roles and experiences.
L8 Use talk to organise, sequence and clarify thinking, ideas, feelings and events.
L9 Hear and say sounds in words in the order in which they occur.
L10 Link sounds to letters, naming and sounding the letters of the alphabet.
L11 Use their phonic knowledge to write simple regular words and make phonetically plausible attempts at more complex words.
L12 Explore and experiment with sounds, words and texts.

L13 Retell narratives in the correct sequence, drawing on language patterns of stories.
L14 Read a range of familiar and common words and simple sentences independently.
L15 Know that print carries meaning and, in English, is read from left to right and top to bottom.
L16 Show an understanding of the elements of stories, such as main character, sequence of events and openings, and how information can be found in non-fiction texts to answer questions about where, who, why and how.
L17 Attempt writing for different purposes, using features of different forms such as lists, stories and instructions.
L18   Write their own names and other things such as labels and captions, and begin to form simple sentences, sometimes using punctuation.
L19 Use a pencil and hold it effectively to form recognisable letters, most of which are correctly formed.

A number of the activities suggested for the theme of 'the Environment' encourage the children to write using their phonic knowledge, develop their vocabularies and recognise words. They have the opportunity to produce posters to encourage people to switch off lights, write postcards from a cold desert and make books about people who live and work in the local environment. Activities using books and playing games such as 'I went to the desert and it was ...' will allow the children to respond in a variety of ways to what they see and hear reinforcing and extending their vocabularies. Throughout all the activities the children should be encouraged to interact and to listen.

Problem Solving, Reasoning and Numeracy (N)

By the end of the EYFS, children should:

N1 Say and use number names in order in familiar contexts.
N2 Count reliably up to ten everyday objects.
N3 Recognise numerals 1 to 9.
N4 Use developing mathematical ideas and methods to solve practical problems.
N5 In practical activities and discussion, begin to use the vocabulary involved in adding and subtracting.
N6 Use language such as 'more' or 'less' to compare two numbers.
N7 Find one more or one less than a number from one to ten.
N8 Begin to relate addition to combining two groups of objects and subtraction to 'taking away'.
N9 Use language such as 'greater', 'smaller', 'heavier' or 'lighter' to compare quantities.
N10 Talk about, recognise and recreate simple patterns.
N11 Use language such as 'circle' or 'bigger' to describe the shape and size of solids and flat shapes.
N12 Use everyday words to describe position.

The theme of 'the Environment' provides a varied context for activities that encourage the children to use numbers, to reason and to solve problems. The opportunity to count occurs as children use the 'Pecking Penguins' and 'Bananas' number rhymes. Children will explore shapes and size as they make exotic, rainforest butterflies and prickly cacti. Children will have the chance to recognise numbers when they play the 'clean up dice game'. Positional language is developed by playing with penguins or polar bears and ice (white boxes) in a cold desert.

Knowledge and Understanding of the World (K)

By the end of the EYFS, children should:

K1 Investigate objects and materials by using all of their senses as appropriate.
K2 Find out about, and identify, some features of living things, objects and events they observe.
K3 Look closely at similarities, differences, patterns and change.
K4 Ask questions about why things happen and how things work.

K5 Build and construct with a wide range of objects, selecting appropriate resources and adapting their work where necessary.
K6 Select the tools and techniques they need to shape, assemble and join materials they are using.
K7 Find out about and identify the uses of everyday technology and use information and communication technology and programmable toys to support their learning.
K8 Find out about past and present events in their own lives, and in those of their families and other people they know.
K9 Observe, find out about and identify features in the place they live and the natural world.
K10 Find out about their environment, and talk about those features they like and dislike.
K11 Begin to know about their own cultures and beliefs and those of other people.

The topic of 'the Environment' offers wonderful opportunities for children to develop their knowledge and understanding of the world as they consider firstly their local environment, and then move on to deserts and rainforests. When exploring the local environment the children are encouraged to consider features that they like and dislike. Activities such as sorting clean rubbish, searching for minibeasts in a hedgerow and pouring water over a pineapple provide the opportunity for the children to make observations and to notice **similarities and differences**. Constructing and **choosing** materials happens as children make quiet shakers and models of bromeliads. ICT plays a valuable part for the children to view penguins, polar bears and a variety of environmental landscapes and features.

Physical Development (PD)

By the end of the EYFS, children should:

PD1 Move with confidence, imagination and in safety.
PD2 Move with control and coordination.
PD3 Travel around, under, over and through balancing and climbing equipment.
PD4 Show awareness of space, of themselves and of others.
PD5 Recognise the importance of keeping healthy, and those things which contribute to this.
PD6 Recognise the changes that happen to their bodies when they are active.
PD7 Use a range of small and large equipment.
PD8 Handle tools, objects, construction and malleable materials safely and with increasing control.

Activities such as using dough and construction toys will offer experience of PD8. Through pretending to walk through a sandy desert or using climbing equipment to role-play being monkeys, builders and window cleaners children will have the opportunity to move with control and imagination. When moving around icebergs (boxes and cones) the children will be encouraged to develop their co-ordination.

Creative Development (C)

By the end of the EYFS, children should:

C1 Respond in a variety of ways to what they see, hear, smell, touch and feel.
C2 Express and communicate their ideas, thoughts and feelings by using a widening range of materials, suitable tools, imaginative and role-play, movement, designing and making, and a variety of songs and musical instruments.
C3 Explore colour, texture, shape, form and space in two or three dimensions.
C4 Recognise and explore how sounds can be changed, sing simple songs from memory, recognise repeated sounds and sound patterns and match movements to music.
C5 Use their imagination in art and design, music, dance, imaginative and role-play and stories.

During this topic children will experience working with a variety of materials as they make models of the local environment, penguins and tidy gardens. They will be able to develop their imaginations and skills of painting, drawing, colouring, cutting and sticking as they make pictures of the local environment, collages of scrap materials, sock-puppet snakes and pictures with sand. Throughout all the activities children should be encouraged to talk about what they see and feel. When singing nursery rhymes and comparing the environments in which they take place the children will explore how sounds can be changed.

Week 1

My environment

Personal, Social and Emotional Development

● Tell the children that their local environment is the area in which they live. Explain that it includes natural things such as trees and also buildings and things added or changed by humans. Having first gained permission from parents, take groups for walks to get a feel for the buildings, plants and other features in their local environment. Record the walk with a digital camera. (PS1, 4)

● Use construction toys and scrap materials to make models of the local environment. Encourage the children to select their own resources. (PS7, 12)

Communication, Language and Literacy

● Make a collection of words to describe the local environment. **Display these with the photos taken** on the walks (see above). (L5)

● Invite children to add a descriptive word to the phrase 'My environment is ...' to make a record-breaking, long sentence (see activity opposite). (L5, 18)

● Make a book about people who live and work in the local environment. Include pictures drawn by the children, photos and descriptions of what the people do. (L11, 17)

Problem Solving, Reasoning and Numeracy

● Use comparative and positional language to describe the size and position of features in the local environment. (N11, 12)

● Work in groups and use card flat shapes to make a picture or plan of the local environment. Encourage the children to name the shapes that they pick to represent buildings, trees, traffic on roads etc. (N11)

Knowledge and Understanding of the World

● Search the book corner for pictures of places similar to the children's local environment. Whilst searching, also draw the children's attention to the variety in environments such as islands, woods and cities. (K9)

● Talk about features in the local environment that are liked and ones that are disliked. Draw pictures

to show both what the environment looks like and, also, possible improvements. (K10)

● Make pictures of buildings found in the local environment. Talk about the materials used to make the buildings. (K9)

Physical Development

● Use clay and mark-making tools to make models of creatures found in the local environment. (PD8)

● Enjoy playing in safe outdoor areas. Encourage the children to realise why particular areas are good for play. (PD1, 2)

Creative Development

● Paint pictures of the local environment. (C3)

● Use boxes, paint and scrap materials to make models of the local environment. (C2)

● Enjoy singing nursery rhymes. After each one talk about the environment in which the rhyme takes place (see activity opposite). (C4)

Activity: Giant Environmental Sentence

Learning opportunity: Collaborating to write and read giant sentences.

Early learning goal: Communication, Language and Literacy. Children should extend their vocabulary, exploring the meanings and sounds of new words. They should… begin to form simple sentences, sometimes using punctuation.

Resources: Flip chart, pens, pencils, strips of plain paper.

Key vocabulary: Environment, sentence, capital letter, full stop.

Organisation: Small group

What to do: Sit with the children on the floor in a circle. Write down the word 'environment'. Help the children to recognise the letters and to say the sounds each one makes. Count the number of 'e' and 'n' letters.

Remind the children what an environment is and ask them to take it in turn to say a word that describes their local environment. As the children to make suggestions and write each one on an A4 piece of paper and lay it on the floor in front of the child who offered the word. When no more ideas are forthcoming, show the group a paper with 'My environment is…' written on. Tell the group that they have just made a very long sentence! Together read it. Say that something is missing from the end of the sentence. Ask how a sentence should start and end. Show the group that their one has a capital letter but needs a full stop. Put one at the end. Finish by re-reading the sentence.

Activity: Nursery Rhyme Environments

Learning opportunity: Exploring well-known nursery rhymes.

Early learning goal: Creative Development. Children should … sing simple songs from memory … and match movements to music.

Resources: Picture book of nursery rhymes.

Key vocabulary: Environment, words within chosen nursery rhymes.

Organisation: Large group

What to do: Show the children the book of nursery rhymes. Invite children to select rhymes for the group to sing.

Sing 'Humpty Dumpty' and look at the illustrations. Encourage the children to use their imaginations as they suggest ideas of where the wall was that Humpty Dumpty sat on and where he lived. As a group describe Humpty Dumpty's local environment.

Help the children to imagine environments for other familiar nursery rhyme characters. If time allows, ask the children to draw pictures to show an environment for a nursery rhyme character chosen by each child. Finish by singing a rhyme and adding actions to the words.

Display

Cover a large board with black paper and a green border strip. At the top in large letters have the phrase 'My environment is …'. On the board display the children's sentences, their paintings and also the photos taken on the walk.

Each morning put out three or four of the models of the local environment on a table. Also, place on it a card showing a lower case letter. Each day ask the children to spy things in the models that start or end with the given letter.

Practical Pre-School Books

Planning
for Learning
through
**The
Environment**

9

Week 2

Taking care of the environment

Personal, Social and Emotional Development

- Talk about the local environment and things that need to be done to take care of it. Make a 'caring hands tree' (see activity opposite). (PS5, 10)
- Talk about the importance of reducing waste, re-using things, recycling and repairing broken items. Help the children to understand why these are important for the environment. (PS9, 10)

Communication, Language and Literacy

- Talk about how switching off lights when we leave a room helps to save energy. Make posters that encourage people to turn off lights. (L17)
- Encourage the children to enjoy using a role-play office made from recycled resources. For example, include paper that is clean on only one side, old diaries, notepads made from scrap paper etc. Encourage the children to tidy the office when they finish playing and to understand the need to take care of the environment. (L7, 11)

Problem Solving, Reasoning and Numeracy

- Use coloured cubes to make towers to show how many children travel to the group's setting walking or by using cars, scooters etc. Talk about which ways are best for the environment and why. (N2, 6)
- Use large photos taken in the local environment for counting practice. How many rubbish bins can be seen? (N1, 2)

Knowledge and Understanding of the World

- Go on a listening walk. (See activity opposite). (K5, 9)
- Make a list of all the animals and plants that can be found in the local environment. Help the children to realise that they need to be 'gentle giants' when near minibeasts and understand how to take care of the plants. (Safety note: All plants should be treated as poisonous unless known otherwise.) (K9)
- Investigate ways to recycle in the local environment e.g. bottle/paper banks. (K9)
- As a group arrange planters with safe bulbs, seeds or plants to brighten an outside area. Look for similarities and differences in the seeds, plants and bulbs. (K1, 3)

Physical Development

- Enjoy being role-play painters. Outside, use large brushes and water to 'paint' walls, the playground and railings in safe areas. (PD8)
- Use climbing equipment to role-play being window cleaners and builders. (PD4, 7)

Creative Development

- Talk about the jobs that need to be done regularly to look after the outsides of buildings. Paint pictures of buildings that have been looked after well. (C2, 3)
- In plastic seed trays make models of gardens that have been looked after well. Encourage the children to collect items from home such as shells, dried flowers, twigs, moss, gravel and bottle tops to place in their gardens. (C2, 5)

Activity: Making A Caring Hands Tree

Learning opportunity: Talking about feelings and considering the needs of themselves and other people.

Early learning goal: Personal, Social and Emotional Development. Children should have a developing awareness of their own needs, views and feelings, and be sensitive to the needs, views and feelings of others. They should consider the consequences of their words and actions for themselves and others.

Resources: A tree trunk made from brown sugar paper; hand sized pieces of paper in leaf colours; pencils, picture of a familiar outside area.

Key vocabulary: Feel, feelings.

Organisation: Whole group introduction, small group practical activity.

What to do: Show the children a picture of an outside area. Talk about the jobs that people do to keep areas pleasant such as emptying bins, outdoor painting, looking after plants etc. Encourage the children to consider what they can do to take care of their environment. Draw round children's hands on plain paper. Cut them out and use them to record the children's ideas for caring. Some children may like to write their own ideas whilst others might simply want to draw a picture. Display the hands as leaves on a tree (see 'Display').

Activity: Making Quiet Shakers

Learning opportunity: Describing sounds and selecting materials to make shakers

Early learning goal: Knowledge and Understanding of the World. Children should select the tools and techniques they need to shape, assemble and join materials they are using. They should observe, find out about and identify features in the place they live…

Resources: Examples of wind chimes, tambourines and shakers; materials to make shakers; rice.

Key vocabulary: Listen, quiet, loud, sound, noise.

Organisation: Whole group introduction, small groups for the practical activity.

What to do: Having received permission from parents to take groups of children on listening walks in the local environment encourage them to listen out for as many different sounds as possible.

Back inside, talk about the variety of sounds. Were there birds? Did anyone hear a car or burglar alarm? Were dogs barking or babies crying? Talk about the difference between pleasant sounds and unwanted noise. Tell the children that they are going to make shakers that, when played, can only just be heard and so would not disturb the people around them.

Ask the children to shut their eyes. Put one piece of rice in a plastic pot and shake it. Ask if anyone can hear something. If they can, ask them to describe the sound. Increase the number of pieces of rice until all can hear a sound. Show a selection of materials that could be used to make shakers. Invite small groups to select their own materials to make shakers.

Display

Cover a board with paper to represent sky and grass. From brown sugar paper cut out a large tree and branches. Show the children how to use sponges and slightly dry paint to give the trunk a bark effect. Display the 'caring hands' as leaves on the tree. Encourage the children to find their own hands and to read what they have written.

Put out the shakers with a selection of nursery rhyme books. During times of free choosing children can enjoy singing the rhymes accompanied by the shakers.

Week 3
Clean up week

Personal, Social and Emotional Development

- Having first gained permission from parents, take groups for walks to look for signs of chewing gum, litter, graffiti etc. Talk about how they make us feel and why we should take care of the area in which we live. (PS8, 9)
- Involve the children in tidying a book corner, sorting crayons or toys, or weeding a safe, garden area. Talk about how it makes the children feel when areas are tidy and organised. (PS5, 9)

Communication, Language and Literacy

- Look through picture books to find pictures of people involved in cleaning. Compare the jobs that they are doing. Enjoy sharing some of the stories. (L1, 3, 4)
- **Put out a selection of toy refuse lorries, plastic figures or dolls and plastic cups as rubbish bins. Invite groups to enjoy being refuse collectors. Encourage the children to make up stories about the lorries and characters. (L7)**

Problem Solving, Reasoning and Numeracy

- Show the children pictures of signs that encourage people not to drop litter and also ones that encourage people to recycle. Invite each child to select a paper shape on which to make their own sign. When completed sort the signs according to their shapes. (N11)
- Play the dice clean-up game (see activity opposite). (N1, 2)

Knowledge and Understanding of the World

- Sort a bin of safe, clean rubbish to find items that could be recycled. Help the children to identify recycling signs and to think of new uses for things that can not be recycled. (K1, 2, 3)
- Draw pictures of new machines to do cleaning (**see activity opposite**). (K7)
- Talk about how composting helps the environment. Make a rota for the children to be 'the group rotters' who collect fruit and vegetable waste during snack times for the compost bin. (K4)
- Investigate a hedge or piece of rotten wood for minibeasts. Help the children to understand the value of hedges and dead wood for the wild life in the environment. (K9)

Physical Development

- Spread 20 beanbags, in a variety of colours around a large space. Challenge the children to 'clean up' the area. (PD4, 7)
- Enjoy using small equipment such as toy irons, dustpans and brushes in the home corner. (PD7)
- Enjoy throwing balls and beanbags into clean rubbish bins. (PD7)

Creative Development

- Use stickers, pictures cut from wrapping paper and recycled signs from safe packaging (e.g. cereal boxes) to decorate large plastic plant pots to be bins for collecting paper to recycle. (C3)
- Make collages with scrap materials. (C3)
- Share a 'Mr Men' or 'Little Miss' story. Paint pictures of a new character – Mr or Miss Clean-up. (C5)

Activity: Dice clean-up game

Learning opportunity: Counting to a given number.

Early learning goal: Problem Solving, Reasoning and Numeracy. Children should say and use number names in order in familiar contexts. They should count reliably up to ten everyday objects.

Resources: Four pieces of A4 paper laminated or small whiteboards, white board pens, a large dice, cleaning cloths.

Key vocabulary: Numbers to ten, clean up, how many?

Organisation: Small group

What to do: Give each child a small whiteboard with pen marks on it. Talk to the children about the importance of taking care of their environment. Explain that it includes leaving areas, toys and equipment as they would like to find them. Show the children the whiteboards with marks and say that they should always be left clean!

Tell the children that they are going to play a game in which they clean the boards. Demonstrate how to shake a die and wipe off that number of marks from a board. Invite the children to take it in turns to shake the die. After each go encourage the children to count how many marks remain. The game finishes when the boards are clean.

Activity: Designing cleaning machines

Learning opportunity: Identifying features of a vacuum cleaner and designing a cleaning machine.

Early learning goal: Knowledge and Understanding of the World. Children should find out about and identify the uses of everyday technology...

Resources: A vacuum cleaner, A4 and A3 white paper, pencils, crayons, boxes, tubes and scrap materials to make models.

Key vocabulary: Clean, machine, vacuum cleaner.

Organisation: Small group

What to do: Remind the children that it is important to take care of the local environment. Talk about the cleaning jobs that have to be carried out both inside and out. Discuss outside jobs such as clearing away leaves in the autumn and inside ones like sweeping carpets.

Show the group a vacuum cleaner. Ask the children what it is and what it does. Help them to notice the switches and where the dust and dirt collects. Explain that you need a small vacuum cleaner for clearing up crumbs after meals and would like them to draw pictures of what one might look like. Show the children some A3 and A4 sized paper and invite each child to select a piece on which to draw their own cleaning machine. If time allows, use the boxes, tubes and scrap materials to make models of the machines.

Display

Around the room put up strips of black paper starting at floor height, as posts for the litter and recycling signs. Place the cleaning machine pictures in plastic wallets and tie them to make an A3 and A4 book. Put out any models of cleaning machines on a piece of carpet. Display the 'Mr Clean Up' paintings on a nearby board.

Week 4

Other environments – Rainforest

Personal, Social and Emotional Development

- Explain to the children what a rainforest is. Show the children pictures. Tell them that the forest is made up of three to four layers and start to make a giant frieze of a rainforest in a corner area to be used for role-play. Over the week add models and pictures of animals and plants (see Knowledge and Understanding of the World and Creative Development.) (PS1, 7)
- Talk about sensible clothes to wear in a rainforest. Paint pictures of rainforest outfits. (PS1, 9)

Communication, Language and Literacy

- Share with the children non-fiction books, pictures and facts about rainforests. Give each child a piece of A4 paper to do a picture and 'write' a sentence about the fact that interested them the most. Use the sheets to make group books about the animals and plants that live in the rainforest. (L17, 18)
- Make a group acrostic for either 'RAIN' or 'RAINFOREST'. Ask the children to suggest something that can be found in the rainforest or a word or phrase to describe the environment for each letter. (L12)
- Make a collection of stories that take place in rainforests. Ask children to select a book to share and to give reasons for their choices. (L3)

Problem Solving, Reasoning and Numeracy

- Enjoy using the banana counting rhyme (see activity opposite). (N2, 5)
- Give children A3 sized flowers and butterflies cut from stiff paper. Ask them to decorate the cut-outs with brightly coloured paper triangles, rectangles, squares and circles. After they are finished encourage the children to use shape and size vocabulary to describe their exotic rainforest butterflies and flowers.(N11)

Knowledge and Understanding of the World

- Show the children pictures of plants that grow in the rainforest. Talk about the 'bromeliad' which is a plant with long, curved leaves that overlap at the base, to make a small bowl which collects water. Make models of bromeliads with plastic drinking cups. (K9)
- Pour water over a large pineapple. Show the children the way that the leaves collect water. Try to grow a pineapple by chopping off the top (leaves and about 2 cm of the pineapple). Leave the top to dry for a few days. Scrape out the fruit and plant the leafy top in soil. Each week observe the plant and look for new leaf growth. (K2)
- Show the children pictures of rainforest plants and/ or an actual plant with waxy leaves. In the water tray enjoy pouring water over a variety of different surfaces. Which ones are like waxy leaves? (K3)

Physical Development

- Encourage the children to be different animals and move in a variety of ways through the rainforest. (PD1, 2, 4)
- Use climbing equipment for the children to be monkeys climbing and swinging in trees. (PD3)

Creative Development

- Make sock puppet snakes (see activity opposite). (C3, 5)
- Make exotic butterflies for a rainforest using finger paint, glitter and decorative scraps. (C3)
- Make fruit bats from felt and card. Hang them at varying heights from a line. (C3)

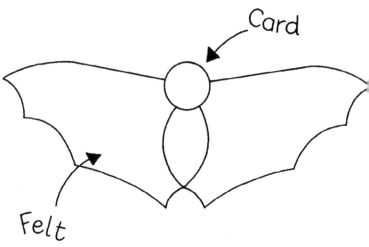

Card

Felt

Planning
for Learning
through
The
Environment

14   Practical Pre-School Books

Activity: Banana number rhyme

Learning opportunity: Using a number rhyme to count, to add and subtract.

Early learning goal: Problem Solving, Reasoning and Numeracy. Children should count reliably up to ten everyday objects. They should, in practical activities and discussion, begin to use the vocabulary involved in adding and subtracting.

Resources: A real banana or a picture of bananas growing in a tree.

Key vocabulary: Numbers to ten, how many, bananas.

Organisation: Large group

What to do: Tell the children that they are going for a walk in the rainforest. Talk about how it feels in the warm, moist atmosphere. Tell them they start to feel like having something for lunch. They look up and see bananas, growing in bunches in a tree. Show the children a real banana or a picture of bananas growing in a tree.

Tell the children to imagine that their fingers are bananas. Recite the number rhyme, miming walking and looking up for bananas, and at the end say 'Let's pick ten'. Ask the children to show you ten bananas (i.e. hold up fingers as if bunches of bananas). Repeat the rhyme for different numbers of bananas. Help the children to realise that different pairs of numbers can produce the same total number (e.g. 3 fingers and 4 fingers, or 5 and 2, could be held up to represent 7 bananas).

Walking in the rainforest what will we see?
Growing at the top of the banana tree.
Lots of bananas hanging up in bunches
How many shall we pick for all our lunches?
Let's pick (insert number).

On further occasions the third and fourth lines could be changed to:

(Insert number) bananas hanging in a bunch,
Let's pick (insert number) to eat for lunch.

The children should then be encouraged to find out how many bananas remain.

Activity: Making and using snake sock puppets

Learning opportunity: Making sock puppets and using them for role-play.

Early learning goal: Creative Development. Children should explore colour, texture, shape, form and space in two or three dimensions. They should use their imagination in art and design… [and] imaginative and role-play.

Resources: Long, plain, clean, no-longer needed socks; decorative materials e.g. sequins, fabric scraps; scissors, PVA glue, pictures of snakes found in a rainforest, felt pens.

Key vocabulary: Snake, puppet

Organisation: Small group

What to do: Look at pictures of snakes that might be found in a rainforest. Encourage the children to look closely at the patterns.

Put a sock over a hand and press the toe in to be a mouth. Tell the children that they are going to make snake sock puppets. Invite them to decorate a sock to be a snake using either felt pens or by sticking on scraps of fabric, sequins and paper shapes. (Tip: When gluing or using pens on the socks insert a piece of scrap card inside to prevent ink or glue going through to the other side.)

Display

Use sugar paper in a variety of shades of green and brown to create a rainforest background with trunks starting at floor level. If possible and safe, hang strips of crepe paper as creepers. Display the fruit bats and butterflies among the trees.

Put out the group rainforest books and a selection of snake puppets on a table covered with green paper or fabric. Set up a line with pegs and letters to spell 'rainforest'. Invite children to enjoy exploring the table resources and rearranging the rainforest letters to make new words.

Week 5

Other environments – Hot deserts

Personal, Social and Emotional Development

● Show the children a picture of a hot desert like the Sahara. Talk about the sand, the heat and the special plants that can be found in a desert. Use the sand tray for groups to role-play visits to a desert. (PS1, 7)

● Talk about the hot days and the cold nights that are typical for a desert climate. Sort a box of clothes into ones suitable for hot days and ones for sleeping in a tent on a cold night. (PS1, 2, 7)

● Talk about sun safety. Dress a doll or a teddy to be protected from the sun. Encourage the children to think about sun cream, covering shoulders and the neck, wearing sunhats, drinking water etc. (PS9)

Communication, Language and Literacy

● Look for pictures of hot deserts in holiday brochures. Help the children to cut some out and to make desert brochures. Encourage them to use their phonic knowledge to write words suck as sand and sun. Use the brochures to role-play being at a travel-agents. (L2, 11)

● In small groups play 'I went to a desert and it was …' (see activity opposite) (L2, 5)

Problem Solving, Reasoning and Numeracy

● Give each child a semi-circle of card and some thin strips of paper to make an eyelid for a camel with ten 'eyelashes'.
Use the eyelids for simple problem solving such as working out how many eyelashes there are on two eyelids and how many are left if the camel loses two lashes. (N5)

● Use flat shapes to make imaginative pictures of prickly cacti. (N11)

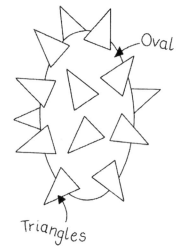

Oval

Triangles

Knowledge and Understanding of the World

● Investigate camel features and select materials for human knee pads (see activity opposite). (K1, 2)

● Invite the children to select from a box of shoes and boots ones suitable for walking on hot sand. Encourage them to give reasons for their choices. (K1, 3)

Physical Development

● Talk about walking on sand. Take the children on a role-play walk in a desert. Encourage them to tread carefully so that they do not sink in the sand. (PD1)

● Use clay to make models of camels. (PD8)

Creative Development

● Paint self-portraits for the title 'Me in a desert'. Encourage the children to consider appropriate clothes for being safe in the sun and for walking on sand. (C3)

● Use wax crayons and finger paints to decorate pieces of A5 folded, stiff card to be tents for protecting desert travelers from the midday sun. (C3)

● Use stiff card, PVA glue and coloured sands to make sandy landscape pictures. (C3)

Activity: Playing 'I went to the desert'

Learning opportunity: Collaborating to play a word game and extending vocabularies.

Early learning goal: Communication, Language and Literacy. Children should enjoy listening to and using spoken and written language, and readily turn to it in their play and learning. They should extend their vocabulary, exploring the meanings and sounds of new words.

Resources: Sand tray, toy plastic camels and people, small card tents.

Key vocabulary: Hot, desert, words suggested by the children.

Organisation: Small – medium group

What to do: Sit with the children in a circle on the floor. Remind them about 'listening eyes' that look at the person who is speaking. Show the children pictures of a hot, sandy desert. Tell the children that they are sitting in the daytime in a very hot desert. Ask them how they feel. Pass a toy camel around the circle and invite each child who holds it to suggest a new word. Collectively try to remember the previous words. Add actions to aid memories. Repeat with different starts to the sentences such as: 'I can see …, 'I can hear …' etc.

Finish by letting small groups use the sand tray as a desert and again encourage the children to use descriptive words for what they see, do and feel.

Activity: Investigating knee pads

Learning opportunity: Finding out about features of camels and comparing materials.

Early learning goal: Knowledge and Understanding of the World. Children should investigate objects and materials by using all of their senses as appropriate. They should find out about, and identify, some features of living things, objects and events they observe.

Resources: A model or picture of a camel; knee-sized samples of a variety of materials e.g. felt, sponge, fur fabric, cotton, imitation leather etc.

Key vocabulary: Camel, hump, names for camel features and materials to be compared.

Organisation: Small group

What to do: Show the children a picture of a camel or a toy one. Explain that there are special reasons why camels can live in hot, sandy deserts. Tell them about the following features. Camels have:

- Three eyelids. The two outer ones have curly, long eyelashes to cover each eye and protect them from sand and the sun. The third, inner eyelid is needed for any dust or sand that might get in.
- Fat stored in the hump that lets a camel survive for long periods of time without food or water.
- Nostrils that can close so sand cannot get in.
- Thick, leathery patches that protect the knees when a camel kneels in hot sand.
- Flat, broad, leathery pads at the bottom of the hooves that prevent the camel from sinking into the sand.

As you discuss each feature, make comparisons with human ones. Invite the children to select materials that would make good kneepads for a human.

Display

Mount the self portraits and sand pictures on brown paper. Display them on a board covered with sand-coloured backing paper. Cover a table with the same coloured paper and set out the clay camels and tents. Place the teddy, dressed for sunny weather, on a small table with a selection of clothes and books depicting a variety of weathers. During times of free choosing the children can enjoy redressing the teddy for different weathers.

Week 6

Other environments – Cold Deserts

Personal, Social and Emotional Development

- Talk about cold deserts. Show the children on a globe where the Arctic and the Antarctic can be found. (PS3)
- Look at pictures to discover which animals live in the Arctic and which ones can be found in the Antarctic. (PS3)
- Practise fastening coats suitable for cold days. (PS11)

Communication, Language and Literacy

- Provide postcards for the children to write and decorate as if on a visit to a cold desert. (L17)
- Play 'I went to the Arctic and I felt …' (see Week 5). Encourage the children to think of descriptive cold words. As a group make a collection of cold words on hexagons cut from white and pale blue card. (L3, 18)

Problem Solving, Reasoning and Numeracy

- Put out three white boxes and three plastic penguins or polar bears. Give the children instructions using size and positional vocabulary of where to move the animals. (N11, 12)
- Use the penguin number rhyme (see activity opposite). (N1, 2)

Knowledge and Understanding of the World

- Investigate melting icebergs in the water tray (made by freezing large plastic tubs or balloons full of water). Safety note: Children should not touch the 'icebergs' with their bare hands. (K1, 3)
- Show the children pictures of clothes to wear in icy conditions. Look at different winter coats. Investigate which coats would be suitable for arctic conditions (see activity opposite). (K1, 3)

Physical Development

- Put out a selection of large boxes or cones that are covered with white paper/fabric. Tell the children that the boxes are large, floating icebergs. Tell a story in which the children are waddling penguins that swim between the icebergs. Describe different ways to move at a variety of speeds and in different directions. (PD1, 2, 3, 4)
- Enjoy running in a safe, outdoor space. Help the children to notice the way they grow hotter when they are active. Remind the children of the different environments that they have met. Talk about the hot and the cold environments. (PD6)
- Make models of polar bears from white dough or clay. (PD8)

Creative Development

- Make penguins from cardboard tubing and coloured paper. Display them with a label that says 'We live in the Antarctic'. (C3)
- Paint polar bears on black paper. Display them with a label that says 'We live in the Arctic'. (C3)

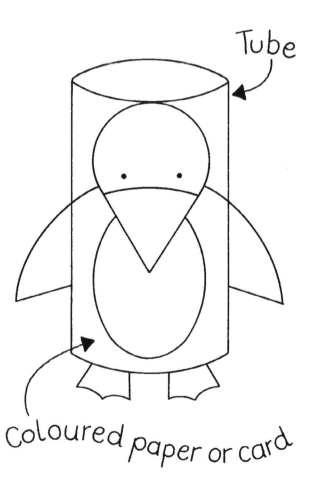

Tube

Coloured paper or card

Activity: Pecking penguin number rhyme

Learning opportunity: Counting and subtracting using a number rhyme.

Early learning goal: Problem Solving, Reasoning and Numeracy. Children should say and use number names in order in familiar contexts. They should count reliably up to ten everyday objects.

Resources: Pictures of different types of penguin e.g. the Adelie penguin.

Key vocabulary: Penguin, numbers to ten, how many.

Organisation: Whole group.

What to do: Show the children pictures of different types of penguin. Tell the children that not all breeds build nests. Explain that Adelie penguins, which can be found in the Antarctic, make nests out of pebbles.

Choose five children to be penguins. Recite the rhyme with the children walking in a circle as if they were penguins. Pick a child to stand on a pebble nest (a piece of card). As a group count how many penguins **stop and rest.**

Tell me, tell me can you see?
Five penguins pecking, sliding free
Over ice and through the snow,
Orange beaks flashing as they go.
One penguin leaves to make a nest
Leaving __ to stop and rest.

For further occasions change the starting number of penguins and/or the number that leave to make a nest.

Activity: Coats for the Arctic

Learning opportunity: Exploring differences in fabrics through looking and touching.

Early learning goal: Knowledge and Understanding of the World. Children should investigate objects and materials by using all of their senses as appropriate. They should look closely at similarities, differences, patterns and change.

Resources: A selection of ski jackets, winter and lightweight coats, pictures of Arctic and Antarctic explorers.

Key vocabulary: Cold, icy, names fro the example coats and fabrics, a storybook set in the Arctic or Antarctic.

Organisation: Small group

What to do: Read a story set in the Arctic or Antarctic. Talk about the environment, the weather and the type of clothes that would need to be worn there. Ask whether anyone has ever been in the snow. What did they wear? Was it cold?

Sort the coats according to criteria such as thick/thin, waterproof/not waterproof, type of fastening. Ask a volunteer to try and fasten a coat whilst wearing gloves or mittens. Which fastenings are easiest to do? As a group make a list of what would be needed for a coat to be suitable for the Arctic or Antarctic. Which coat matches the list best?

Display

Cover a board with white paper on which to display the polar bear pictures. In front place a table covered with a white sheet or paper. Put a second table nearby. On one place a label to say 'Arctic' and on the other 'Antarctic'. Involve the children in helping to display the penguins and polar bears on the correct tables. In addition invite the children to select storybooks that have penguins or **polar bears as central characters to add to the displays.** Finish by asking the children to make name labels using 'cold colours' for their animals.

Cover a second board with white paper. Use red, shiny paper to make a picture of a postbox. Display the postcards as if tumbling out of the box.

Bringing It All Together - The Environmental Patchwork Day

The Environmental Patchwork Day is a creative way to finish a project on 'the Environment'. It can lead to the production of one or more beautiful pieces of artwork to which all children contribute. Children and parents will feel proud when they see the work displayed. In addition the patchwork will be a lasting memory for important messages learnt over the project.

Preparation

At the start of the topic send out a letter to parents seeking volunteers to help on the Patchwork Day. Explain that adults are needed to work with pairs or small groups of children to make patchwork pieces. Tell them that the theme of the pieces will be on protecting the environment.

Prepare the children for the day, by looking back over the topic, and remembering the different types of environments that they have considered. Talk about the importance of looking after all our environments so that all animals, including people, can appreciate them and survive. Talk about the different climates and the types of animals and plants that live in each area.

Resource requests

Ask all parents to provide an old shirt or overall in a named bag for their child to wear on the Patchwork Day. Also ask for contributions of food for an environmental snack. This might include 'polar' ice-pops or lollies, penguin or butterfly shaped biscuits, or fruit from a rainforest area. If there are child-friendly foods associated with the local environment try to get contributions of those too.

Environmental Patchwork Day

On the day set out a number of tables with resources to make square patchwork pieces. (Squares of around 10 cm x 10cm work well.) All the squares should be the same size so that they can be combined easily in a patchwork. Each piece should focus on one environment. As the children work they should be encouraged to think about the environment and to consider why it is important to take care of all environments.

The patchwork pieces could be based on the following techniques:

- Roll out clay and, press in and remove leaves and other natural objects found in the local environment to leave an imprint. When dry the pieces can be glued onto a large piece of hardboard and varnished.
- Use fabric crayons on squares of white cotton cut from an unwanted, clean sheet.
- Make collages on felt squares using fabric scraps, sequins and glue.
- Make paper collage patchwork pieces. The squares could show a scene or be abstract ones showing either cool or hot colours made by gluing on paper pieces cut from colour supplement magazines.
- Use pastels and cotton wool balls to smudge and combine colours to make landscapes.
- Stick natural objects such as shells, stones, leaves and twigs on stiff card. Varnish with watered down PVA glue.

As the squares are completed lay them, temporarily, on tables so that the children can see the patchworks taking form. Finish the day by sharing the donated food and reinforcing the message of taking care of the environment.

Invite parents to help in the final presentation of the patchworks. Glue the pottery ones onto a piece of hardboard and display flat on a table. Laminate the paper squares and mount them onto a large piece of thin card. Display the fabric pieces by stitching them together on a sheet. Border the pieces with ribbon.

Planning
for Learning
through
The
Environment

20   Practical Pre-School Books

Resources

Resources to collect:
- Small composting bin
- Toy camels, penguins and polar bears
- World globe
- A pineapple
- Plastic seed trays
- Shells
- Dried flowers
- Gravel
- Old diaries
- Coloured cubes
- Planters, potting compost and depending on the time of year, safe seeds, plants and/or bulbs.
- Winter coats showing a variety of materials, fastenings and weights.
- Different types of footwear
- Coloured sands

Everyday resources:
- Boxes e.g. cereal packets, shoe boxes
- Variety of papers and cards e.g. sugar, tissue, silver and shiny papers, wallpaper, corrugated card, etc.
- Paint, different sized paintbrushes and a variety of paint mixing containers
- Pencils, crayons, pastels, felt pens etc.
- Glue and scissors
- Decorative and finishing materials such as sequins, foils, glitter, tinsel, shiny wool and threads, beads, pieces of textiles, parcel ribbon
- Table covers
- Malleable materials such as play-dough and clay
- Masking tape
- Containers to make shakers
- Rice
- Cardboard tubes
- Cones
- Sand and water trays
- Green border strip
- Beanbags

All of the following books were available from leading booksellers at the time of writing. When planning for the topic, however, look through the books already within your setting. It is likely that you will have many books that depict a wide range of environments which would be equally useful.

Story books
- Giles Andreae *Rumble in the Jungle* (Hachette Children's Books)
- Elizabeth Baguley *A Long Way from Home* (Little Tiger Press)
- Eileen Browne *Handa's Surprise* (Walker Books)
- Julia Donaldson *A Squash and a Squeeze* (Macmillan)
- Julia Donaldson *Monkey Puzzle* (Macmillan)
- Julia Donaldson *The Smartest Giant in Town* (Macmillan)
- Roger Hargreaves *Mr. Bump - Mr. Men Classic Library* (Egmont Books Ltd)
- Shirley Hughes *The Big Alfie Out of Doors Story Book* (Red Fox)
- John Prater *The Big Dark* (Red Fox)

Non-fiction books
- Ruth Brocklehurst *1001 Animals to Spot* (Usborne Publishing Ltd)
- Katie Daynes & Peter Allen *See Inside Planet earth* (Usborne Publishing Ltd)

Rhymes and Songs
- Lucy Cousin's *Big Book of Nursery Rhymes* (Macmillan Children's Books)
- *First Picture Nursery Rhymes* illustrated by Jo Litchfield (Usborne Publishing Ltd)
- *Five Little Monkeys* by Zita Newcome (Walker Books)

Resources for planning
- *The Early Years Foundation Stage: Setting the Standards for Learning, Development and Care for children from birth to five* (Department for Education and Skills)
- For additional ideas for activities that link with the theme of the environment see the following titles within the *Planning for Learning* Series (Practical Pre-School Books): *Recycling Where I live*

Collecting Evidence of Children's Learning

Monitoring children's development is an important task. Keeping a record of children's achievements, interests and learning styles will help you to see progress and will draw attention to those who are having difficulties for some reason. If a child needs additional professional help, such as speech therapy, your records will provide valuable evidence.

Records should cover all the areas of learning and be the result of collaboration between group leaders, parents and carers. Parents should be made aware of your record keeping policies when their child joins your group. Show them the type of records you are keeping and make sure they understand that they have an opportunity to contribute. As a general rule, your records should form an open document. Any parent should have access to records relating to his or her child. Take regular opportunities to talk to parents about children's progress. If you have formal discussions regarding children about whom you have particular concerns, a dated record of the main points should be kept.

Keeping it manageable

Records should be helpful in informing group leaders, adult helpers and parents and always be for the benefit of the child. The golden rule is to keep them simple, manageable and useful.

Observations will basically fall into three categories:
- **Spontaneous records:** Often you will want to make a note of observations as they happen e.g. a child is heard counting cars accurately during a play activity, or is seen to play collaboratively for the first time.

- **Planned observations:** Sometimes you will plan to make observations of children's developing skills in their everyday activities. Using the learning opportunity identified for an activity will help you to make appropriate judgments about children's capabilities and to record them systematically.

To collect information:
- talk to children about their activities and listen to their responses;
- listen to children talking to each other;
- observe children's work such as early writing, drawings, paintings and 3D models. (Keeping photocopies or photographs can be useful.)

Sometimes you may wish to set up 'one off' activities for the purposes of monitoring development. Some groups at the beginning of each term, for example, ask children to write their name and to make a drawing of themselves to record their progressing skills in both co-ordination and observation. Do not attempt to make records following every activity!

- **Reflective observations:** It is useful to spend regular time reflecting on the children's progress. Aim to make some comments about each child each week.

Informing your planning

Collecting evidence about children's progress is time consuming and it is important that it is useful. When you are planning, use the information you have collected to help you to decide what learning opportunities you need to provide next for children. For example, a child who has poor pencil or brush control will benefit from more play with dough or construction toys to build the strength of hand muscles.

Example of recording chart

Name: Lucy Field		D.O.B. 17.2.05		Date of entry: 13.9.08		
Term	**Personal, Social and Emotional Development**	**Communication, Language and Literacy**	**Problem solving, Reasoning and Numeracy**	**Knowledge and Understanding of the World**	**Physical Development**	**Creative Development**
ONE	Happy to say good-bye to mother. Enjoys both independent and collaborative play. 20.9.08 LBS	Enjoyed looking through books for different environments. Can write first name and simple CVC words. Good pencil grip. 2.10.08 CCM	Is able to say and recognise numbers to ten and to count accurately five objects. Enjoyed counting bananas in the rhyme. 25.9.08 EHL	Very eager to ask questions always wants to know 'Why?' Keen to learn about animals and plants in a rainforest. Fascinated by the camel facts 16.10.08 LSS	Very flexible. Can balance on one leg. Loved miming walking in a desert. Good at aiming. Does not like the feel of clay. 9.10.08 SJS	Enjoys painting and particularly when mixing own colours. Sand picture showed attention to detail. Not keen to get hands messy. 22.10.08 REL
TWO						
THREE						

Skills overview of six-week plan

Week	Topic Focus	Personal, Social and Emotional Development	Communication, Language and Literacy	Problem Solving, Reasoning and Numeracy	Knowledge and Understanding of the World	Physical Development	Creative Development
1	My environment	Showing interest and feelings; Selecting resources independently; Forming good relationships	Extending vocabulary; Using phonic knowledge to write words; Using simple punctuation	Recognising and describing shapes; Comparing sizes; Using positional language	Finding out about and identifying features; Discussing likes and dislikes of local features	Moving with control, co-ordination, imagination and in safety; Using small equipment and malleable materials	Painting; Cutting and sticking; Singing
2	Taking care of the environment	Considering consequences; Understanding what is right and wrong and why; Being aware of personal and others' feelings	Writing; Using phonic knowledge to write words; Role-play	Counting; Comparing numbers	Finding out about and identifying features; Observing; Comparing; Selecting tools and techniques; Constructing	Showing awareness of space and others; Handling tools with control and safely; Using small equipment	Painting; Making models
3	Clean up week	Understanding what is right and wrong and why; Being aware of personal and others' feelings	Listening; Interacting; Making up stories	Counting; Recognising and describing shapes	Observing; Comparing; Asking questions; Finding out about and identifying features in the natural world	Showing awareness of space and others; Aiming; Using small equipment	Collage; Cutting and sticking
4	Other environments – Rainforest	Showing interest; Forming good relationships; Understanding what is right and wrong and why	Listening; Writing; Exploring words	Counting; Using the vocabulary of addition and subtraction; Recognising and describing flat shapes	Comparing; Investigating; Constructing	Moving with control, co-ordination, imagination and in safety; Using large equipment	Making puppets; Finger painting; Cutting and sticking
5	Other environments - Hot deserts	Being confident to try new activities; Speaking; Initiating ideas; Understand what is right and wrong and why	Writing; Speaking; Listening; Extending vocabulary; Using phonic knowledge	Recognising flat shapes; Counting; Using the vocabulary of addition and subtraction	Investigating; Observing; Talking	Moving with imagination; Using malleable materials	Painting; Sticking; Colouring
6	Other environments - Cold deserts	Maintaining attention; Dressing and undressing independently	Using phonic knowledge to write words; Listening	Counting; Using language for size and position	Investigating; Comparing	Moving with control, co-ordination, imagination and in safety; Recognising body changes after activity; Using malleable materials	Painting; Cutting and sticking; Making models

Home links

The theme of environments lends itself to useful links with children's homes and families. Through working together children and adults can gain respect for each other and build comfortable and confident relationships.

Establishing Partnerships
- Keep parents informed about the topic of 'Environments' and the themes for each week. By understanding the work of the group, parents will enjoy the involvement of contributing ideas, time and resources.
- Photocopy the parent's page for each child to take home.
- Invite parents to help to run the Environmental Patchwork Day and enjoy viewing the finished results.

Visiting Enthusiasts
- Invite known adults who work in the local environment to talk to the children about what they do.
- Invite parents to talk about how they care for the local environment.
- Invite the person/people who clean the group's setting to talk about the types of jobs they do each day and ones that are done less often. Encourage the children to consider how they can help to take care of their environment.

Resource Requests
Ask parents to donate:
- Postcards and pictures of the local environment, as well as deserts and rainforests;
- No longer needed winter coats;
- Food for the Environmental Patchwork Day;
- Materials for the patchworks.

The Environmental Patchwork Day
It is always useful to have extra adults at times such as the Environmental Patchwork Day. Involve them in helping to run the patchwork activities and in the setting out and serving of the food.

After the Environmental Patchwork Day, give parents who were unable to help on the day, the opportunity to help in the completion of the patchworks.